Earth Science

Earth Science

{ PAM CLEMENTS }

Earth Science
Copyright © 2013 by Pam Clements

All rights reserved. No part of this book may be used or reproduced in any form, electronic or mechanical, including photocopying, recording, or scanning into any information storage and retrieval system, without written permission from the author except in the case of brief quotation embodied in critical articles and reviews.

Cover design by The Troy Book Makers
Book design by The Troy Book Makers
Printed in the United States of America

The Troy Book Makers • Troy, New York • thetroybookmakers.com

To order additional copies of this title, contact your favorite local bookstore or visit www.tbmbooks.com

ISBN: 978-1-61468-178-6

For Peg and Joe

who taught us how
to look and listen

Acknowledgments

Several poems have appeared in the following journals, newspapers, and anthologies:

Association of Franciscan Colleges and Universities Journal: "Spoonbills."

Black Petals: "Event Horizon," "Mars Dream."

Blue line: "Autumn," "Garnet."

Buffalo News: "Ice Age."

Celebrations (July Literary Press): "Wodewose."

Dan River Anthology: "Bond," "Geodes."

Earth's Daughters: "First Dive," "Obsidian," "River Road," "Things Seen Along the Thruway," "What the Spider Said."

Emrys: "Salamander"

Hidden Oak Poetry Journal: "Loon Warden."

Icon: "Concretions," "Geodes."

Kalliope: "Granite."

Oriel: "Fredonia Harvest."

Pyramid Lake Anthology 2009: "Solstice."

Red Owl Magazine: "Canoe."

Salvage: "Dad's Meteorite."

Timber Creek Review: "Maple."

" Like the rock shop owner in causing readers to notice what we pass by too quickly. In her poem "Geodes," Pam Clements splits open the possibilities of multiple hemispheres and strata as insights emerge from the places she writes about – refracting light on the details. Her poems are studies of both the familiar and the unobserved, causing readers to notice what is passed by too quickly. She is an intuitive observer, risking openness, embracing her past, and immersing herself in the large and small aspects of nature's seasons. Her girlhood curiosity remains alive with a mature ironic eye. "

Joyce Kessel, author of *Secret Lives* and an editor of *Earth's Daughters*

" Pam Clements is poet whose exquisite observations always lead to the elemental, sometimes through metaphors stunningly clear in their finite sureness, but often through associations made so deftly you hardly notice until you have arrived at the other thing: granite's hardness, the elusive meteorite, the inevitable frost. Each of these poems takes on that inevitability, making us think, at their end, that we knew what the poet has shown us, all along, even as they open our eyes again and again. These poems are gifts that Clements gives us like a found fossil or observed layer in the rock walls of our lives. "

Nate Leslie, author of seven books of poetry, including *Salvaged Maxims, Egress, and Small Cathedrals*

" In this collection, Clements startles and delights, from the cool geologic poems to the jolt of profound, personal musings. She highlights creatures of all kinds: salamanders and sea turtles, spoonbills and spiders. You nearly faint from sheer abundance. And yet these creatures are not the stars. Her memories are the stars, the force that tries to whisk you easily into free fall. A very satisfying read from a grounded poet, sure-footed, but with wings to catch the ever-present wind. "

Mimi Moriarty, author of *War Psalm*, *Sibling Reverie* and *Crows Calling*

Table of Contents

1. Shadows
2. Garnet
3. Canoe
4. Loon Warden
6. Charity Event
7. Shale
8. Obsidian
9. Bond
10. Things Seen Along the Thruway
12. Granite
14. Maple
15. Style
16. Autumn
17. Chert
18. Blood Drive
19. Concretions

21. Event Horizon
23. Mars Dream
24. Gift
25. Dad's Meteorite
26. Geodes
28. Salamander
29. First Dive
30. Spoonbills
31. Wodewose
33. What the Spider Said
34. The Earl of Autumn
36. Fredonia Harvest
38. Arrowhead
40. Solstice
41. The Element Carbon
42. Cenozoic
44. Samhain
45. Liquidity
46. River Road
48. Ice Age

Shadows

like a blind man

grasp images

shadowed and sure

flapping shutter

chirping girl,

a wrenching spirit

under the eaves

warning the waves

over heart

over stone

but under black pearl

Garnet

Once, as a girl
In a long abandoned mine
I found a garnet
The color of clotted blood
As big as my fist.
Fractured by crevices
Ready to sliver,
Fall into fragments
Too much like my teenaged life.

Somehow, it held,
Came out of the matrix
Whole, unkempt,
Awkward as I was
Wielding a chisel
And helplessly waiting
To get back in the car
So we could drive and drive,
Songs on the radio always
Telling me
What it might mean to be cool.

Canoe

Scrapes on sand
as we push off into
Eighth Lake
for one full day
of easy paddling.

It hugs the shore
where dying trees
leer over water, leafless, eerie.
Already fallen trunks,
submarine, touch our hull
with ghastly fingers.

Achieves Bug Cove, a shallow bog
hemmed with reeds,
rife with liles – yellow cow-eye globes,
pink or white mandalas –
It rustles through a skim
of cloven, frog-foot leaves;
mosquitos rise and bite.
We pull away, alarm a muskrat
some few feet
ahead as we slip past.

Loon Warden

For Liz

One summer she lived among loons,
sleeping in an open shed
on Ragged Island
warning burr-engined boaters
away from nests.

In the boat
from celadine dawn to purple shadow
watching chicks ride
their parents' black backs,
lake waxen under heavy mist,
trailing a black glissando.

The loons become, like her
eloquent on water,
improbable on land
sprawled in stick nests.
She thinks of herself and them as one
with the cool tannic
smell of lake water,
pitch of pine tar.

At night,
jade Buddha
she sits up in her sleeping bag
attending to
their hard-wired
weird, high
ululating
green-tinged
grief-stricken
calls.

Charity Event

Brassy cubes
Of American cheese
Balance like pueblos,
Like a painting by Legère,
Crowning a plate
More expensive
Than my first car.

Careful art
Lines the walls; music
Percolates in air.
The best champagne
Sizzles in crystal.
Damasked and courted
As Medici, donors
Swan the surface tension
Of the ballroom
In austere black and gold.

Representing hoi polloi
I venture to amuse.
Donors nod importantly.
Brassy crystals jut
In lumpen granite.

We really need this bequest
Without question
Our cause is good.
But we seed it every season
With the greenish dye-job sheen
Of pyrite crystals.

Shale

A file of pale destroyers
pushes past the harbor,
past the Battery,
past pyramids of fused shot,
cannonade of earlier battles.

Those bristling ships
a smear of shale clay,
step by misstep
we settle into war
as the farce of diplomacy sinks
into long flat layers
of lies
this time of day
when there is no horizon.

Off the promenade rail
oyster catcher bills
the color of traffic cones,
the Navy's crenellated ships
fade gray to gray,
pelicans aweather.

Obsidian

Your greatest yearning –
to believe
to get a little mystical,
pull in messages
from table-rappings,
crop circles,
prayer,
and still remain your own cool self.

Your leather jacket, igneous,
reflects, (moonlight on waves,
ghost-soldiers marching north to Charleston
crackling coquinas
along the beach)
glints from
your rimless Emma Goldman specs
from your camera lens
curved concave
as the hollow in your chest,
space left for desire.

Dark lava flash-cooled
flung into the world
to gloss sharp black,
your eye measures loss.

Bond

Easing the shore
to silence
aluminum scrape on sand
Owl Mountain greenblack night
willing the canoe
adrift
so no one could descry
us on the lake at midnight.

Conspirators
waiting for a beacon,
lying head to foot
along chill metal
stars pressed close
gas-bright
grackle-winged.

With you I have
been brave. With you
I leap to risk.
When the sky opens
for meteor flash
I am your right-hand girl.

Things Seen Along the Thruway

1. Forty-three groundhogs
   feed, noses down
   or up, smelling moist air
   one Easter weekend.

2. After an ice storm, tractor trailors
   jackknifed, glazed and still,
   lie bent like sleepers, arms crooked under their heads.

3. White fog, shoulder-high
   lines the Mohawk;
   deer heads curve up, sniff, then
   down, disappear,
   rising, dropping
   into ivory shadows –
   a Chinese painting.

4. Ten hot red taillights
   line the back of a semi:
   guide in a blizzard.

5. Squads of serious boys in camouflage
    ride looking only ahead
    in convoy of squat
    olive jeeps
    from the last war.

6. Between towns, willows
    tilt into the river.
    Abandoned canal locks,
    broken tannery windows,
    fields of yesterdays.

7. Nothing.

    One summer of illness and death
    of too many trips across the state to count
    road cuts shedding
    sediment in rock flakes –
    Promises, promises.

8. A runway's blue lights
    fade into distance;
    jet wheels clank down
    fifty feet over your head
    Coming into Buffalo.

Granite

When I came home
From kindergarten announcing
My ambition to become a nurse,
She whirled around from chopping,
Pointed a serrated knife at me, and growled,
"Don't you want to be a DOCTOR?"
I got a stethoscope.

When she found me sobbing
Over Beth's last hours in Little Women,
She snapped, "If you don't stop weeping,
I'll take that book away
And you'll never know how the story ends."
I gulped back tears.

One summer, camping,
We got stuck in an alfalfa field.
She gunned the old black Ford
Out of the muck, flew clear to the road
Came down hard on Canadian granite
Cracking the oil pan,
The rest of us running to catch up.
She bought a gold convertible.

When I approached with news
Of a college boyfriend,
Chopping again, she bellowed,
"Marriage? Not until you're thirty-five!"
Laughing, I returned to my studies.

When I achieved thirty-five, still single,
Drinking late at night together,
From deep in her customary chair, she roared,
"Get thee to a sperm bank!
Or better still, adopt an orphaned child."
I consulted bank account and options.

I tried to take each turn
She would have taken
In my stead
But still collided with
The solid bedrock
She tried so hard to undermine.

Maple

I own a tree
an aged maple
shading the entire back yard
quilting it with leaves each fall,
with seeds each spring.

No, I own the rights
to a square of property
on which an ancient
black maple tree resides
sharing its last years
with my household.

But no, again, perhaps I own
merely the right to sit
watching the twilight
open to the first stars
beneath the spreading branches of
one venerable tree.

Style

Banded: rings of Saturn
Agate, or a wave-lapped shore
lobed and multiple
multivarious, solitary malachite.
The stance: opulence, precision, elegance
a little black dress of minerals.

All greens lap in rounded lobes
fern glades in green-black-gray,
parakeet backs
tongues of green
asparagus al dente
opaque emerald
beer bottle drift-glass
striated, coruscated
bunched in rock, layered as lichen nodes.

Nodes, lobes
The color connotes style.

Mineral love
sexual as difference
the cold that tempers heat
just before the needle point
of ecstasy.
Cool as intellect
depth that submits to polish
But will not shine.

Autumn

Tart taste
of salt and cinnamon
savories — a hint
of cider in the air
with sharp mold-crush of red oak leaves
making noise
beneath our sneakers.
Early dark
ushers russet evenings
and doughy sleep at last
in night-cool bedrooms
after August's dank
mildewed humidity.
As the first Canadian front
seeps east-southeast
all senses finally awake
as the air clears
to lemon and ginger,
in mirror-polished sky
Orion rising.

Chert

The edge of February
slips through flesh
dun winds
flirt flint,
wind
gone concave
as an apple core.
The hammer of duty
chips at your temple
the pressure of a question.

Your history
settles round you
layer by layer,
greasy, conchoidal:
your mother's death,
your father's disappointment,
your grandmother's religion.
Secure as a nut
in its burr,
as a fossil in matrix
you waited eons
for someone with just the right chisel
to chip into your world.

This sedimentary century
tells you what to expect
when you emerge,
cicada,
blinking and screaming
at the light.

Blood Drive

Hematite:
The seasonal sacrifice
given a bike handle
to squeeze
pinch sting
buzz of fluorescent lights.
Holes in ceiling tiles
slow draw and drip
a bag of iron oxide
metamorphic,
necessary as the earth's crust
and orange juice after

Concretions

Concretions: "Roughly spherical or rounded, more or less symmetrical structures in clastic sedimentary rocks; concretions are formed by the accumulations and concentration of mineral matter... around a nucleus (often a fossil) in the approximate center of the structure."

-Audubon Society Field Guide to North American Rocks and Minerals

She sits on the edge
of the too-high table
in the room too subtly green,
paper crackling beneath her,
ominous, anatomical,
torn between wondering
whether she'd made paper
wrinkle too much
and what kind of sediment
has settled around
the approximate clastic center
of her structure.

She has felt such
roughly spherical lobes before
beneath her mother's flesh,
marble swellings
as if some mineral matter
had dropped through cells
to concentrate and harden.

Thirty years ago
she and the other children
would troop "down the gully"
to Stony Acres'
deep dim creekbed
home of crayfish, minnows, spotted efts
lurking under rounded rocks
slick with moss.
They called them "turtlebacks,"
old concretions
crossed by cracks
rounded into fossil humps
by freshets every spring.

Crumpling the paper,
she thinks back to that greenness
fern-fringed, matted trails
leading down, then up again
filtered light on leaf compost.
She remembers her old friend David's
scuffed white boots,
red cowboy hat,
keen eye for crawfish or deer print.

She wonders if she'll be a good patient.
She is not patient.
But enraged
at these concretions,
this sedimentary effluvia
hardening into rounded lobes –
the effrontery of it –
the betrayal
of nature deep within.

Event Horizon

Event horizon:
a space/time spot at which
light escapes
the pendulous philosophic gravity
of a black hole.

I have known a few potential suicides
but only one who
called me up at four am
asking me to pull him back
from inevitability.

Jarred awake on the futon
on the floor of my Carolina slave house
pretending not to hear
palmetto bugs
scuttling the cat's dish downstairs –
I always pick up.

Blind without glasses or light,
without wine or cigarettes,
I hold him on the line
for hours,
making sure he's bandaged his wrists,
eliciting promises
to call a hot line
from a thousand miles away.

Facing utter dark
eyeless, thirsty,
locusts buzzing beyond the porch,
how long have I known
it would come to this, to
you, bleeding and crying, with
me at the edge of the cataract,
pulling against the force
that tries to whisk you easily
into free fall.

Mars Dream

Red dust dream planet
confronts sleep:

A desperate plain, scoured oxide brown.

Three black crouched figures
On steep iron cliffs
Perch above desert river.

Contained, you are distant
As this withered arroyo,
erosion your only principle.
Knees to your chest, you emanate cold,
shift against gravel, restless.

Atmosphere, a chemical wash, silent
as rusting old metal,
wars with canyon rims.
Your eye shoots glass across scree.

You sit with two shadows,
one I know well;
blackened, crooked as cormorants
you smile like reptiles.

It was a deaf dream and rock-dry dream as well.
Red dust still scrubs my teeth.

Gift

A chain of stars has been your gazing gift.
You woke me up to witness Northern Lights:
red panels swung across my sky, a shift
of waves of fire that tangled in my sight.
Space-science brought you satellites and stars;
binoculars, your vigil's only tool.
You taught me how to look at planets' scars
though cold dawn-risings made you comet's fool.
You've never lost the mystery of the skies
beyond this cosy atmosphere of earth;
for you, the pattern and the meaning lies
beyond our scope, our telescopes, our birth.
Your gift is knowledge laced with wonder, framed
By awe of infinite, delighted, unashamed.

Dad's Meteorite

Was always
Going to fall
But never did, unless
He was looking sideways
At something else,
A nighthawk's wing,
A skunk in the bushes.
A clump of partridge berry.
Each time, one surgeon-stroke of light
Incised the sky
And then was gone
Before he ever could define it.

Geodes

In the rock shop
they sit like tennis balls
lumped in a basket
unceremonious, gray, cheap,
mounded like meatballs
something for children.

Sometimes the rock shop owner
offers to cut one in half
so you will have two hemispheres
fanged with crystals
to carry home,
or to chisel a hole, trepanning,
revealing treasure, a Faberge egg
sculpted of rock.

A space emerges
in the strata
dissolved by hydrochloric rainwater
replete with minerals
that frost the margin
in solid distillation.

As memories erode
within the brain
gaps appear, along with clarity
as if some weak acid
has distilled the past
changing sediment to
crystal
a hollow within.

Salamander

A winter of cold birds.
The creek at the corner winds
underground, twists off towards Hudson
away from my affections.
Bluff-torn, battered, we stand
stamping,
looking into cold water,
hands in our pockets.
In this cold season
you will never know
what might be moving small and slow
beneath the ice, what strange creature
hibernates under frostbound rock,
what trilobite or salamander
lumbers ever after you.

First Dive

The squat dive boat shelters
in a coral cove.
We take last direction,
adjust masks and snorkels,
go over the side
into the sound of our own breathing.

The reef impossibly beneath us,
farms lapis broccoli and kale.
We fan out flat and wide.
Yellow tangs swirl like glitter,
The world a moving jewel
A Moorish idol vamps us.
Parrotfish bite the reef itself,
stab coral dust puffs.

Transported, transfixed
we hang like crucifixes
looking down and down

One green-plated sea turtle
pulls itself from below
the reef paws at water,
its eyes unaware
of our still watching.
It climbs / dives up
out of the Cretaceous
moves among divers,
turns west,
palms downward, beak open,
sinks deliberately into blue.

Spoonbills

Brakelight angels,
liminal creatures
stepping to feed at the verge
between seagrass and water,
distant, unconcerned, as hard to believe
as if three unicorns were to step daintily
onto this Texas highway, nosing at roadkill.

Such improbable animals,
shrimp-pink, awkward,
those spatulate bills
not unlike the spoons
opticians hand you, telling you
"Now, cover your left eye."

Heavy heads swing from side to side,
sieve protein out of silt
eyes rolling, dowagers aghast at scandal.

Heat blurs the apparition
but we watch and watch
until they launch themselves aloft
akimbo, blushing,
assured as adolescent princesses.

Wodewose

A trail well marked
through second-growth forest,
lean sassafrass trees flirt/flash yellow mittens,
loam sponges underfoot
with moist smell
of death recycling.
Off trail, old oaks hung with cabled vines
lumped with shelf fungus: something winks.
Hint of a smile
where the green man resides
lies abundance

Wodewose, wild man of the woods
runs mad with his beard of moss;
whatever he touches, grows:
star moss, dogtooth violets, partridge berry
Indian pipes spring from his step.
Just a pair of eyes a glint in ivy
vanishing.

Hildegarde called it veriditas
greening, freshening
spiritual fecundity, union with nature
by which she meant the cosmos, everything
living and dying beneath eyes of the woods;
stump turns to loam, leaf-mold to mushroom food.

The green man
plumps, dampens, makes seedpods burst
dirt in his fingernails, grit
in the creases of his hewn face.
He is Lord of Kudzu
and Dandelion,
of crabgrass, kelp cities,
wild grapevines, honeysuckle tangling the fences,
of lichens clasped to arctic rock,
the twinkle
of plenitude.

What the Spider Said

I sing my own song
gargle gossamer into being.

My webs brush your leg
when you least expect me.

I signify neglect
hidden, forgotten corners.

The universe is made of patterns.
I secrete one

I keep a pantry
provisions hermetically sealed.

I sail on wind and whisker
scrabbling my own lines.

I taught fishers to make nets
and how to knit.

My hunting and my art:
two parts of the same puzzle.

The Earl of Autumn

As ever
he arrives
at the cemetery's shallow pond
at first late-summer
leaf-turn.
The oaks boast a little rust; one or two
red leaves appear.

Shagbark feathers
slate-colored,
curve towards the water.

He waits
immobile
expectant
of small prey below,
gutbucket bullfrogs belching.

His steps
precise as a vicar's,
frock coat tattered,
brow wide, his
eye discerning.

Alert to the presence
of the dog,
he gives us
the eye sardonic
then knees himself
upward
neck pulled in like a prow
to preen on pine branch
glowering,
royally offended,
resenting the interruption
of such easy pickings.

Fredonia Harvest

You could trail out of town
following Canadaway Creek
into old vineyards where
after the harvest
no one would mind
if you picked, pinched, or ate
bunches too strong
for mechanical paddles.

Vervain, brown burdock
rise between rows
of purpling leaves;
burrs cling to your jeans.

You could carry
grapes in your backpack
enough for a batch of jam
gifts from your gleaning.

Downstream, a path
angles into woods, red-gold
sumac and sycamore. A log
has fallen exactly where
it makes sense to sit, laden,
watch down the gully
through quivering leaves,
water rushing over
turtlebacks, trout sleeping
and, alone in the wind
you nearly faint
from sheer abundance.

Arrowhead

Eastham's beaches
arch the bay to east and west,
the Tower a mere gray needle.
Still.

The bay is still,
sky the color of cedar shakes.
Receding tide reveals a mile or more
of clam flats, sawgrass hummocks
green as limes.

Walking the rock and kelp line, it appears
among familiar drift:
skates' egg cases, moon snail collars,
a perfect scallop shell.
Surprise – a gleam of flint
chipped carefully
an arrowpoint
no larger than my thumb.

I pick it up – bone-white, still sharp
Micmac? Narragansett?
washed from dunes last winter.
Still on this strange knot-fisted arm of land
flexing the Atlantic,
thin-chipped reminder

that tribes of bathing families,
flocks of revelers in P-town bars,
in future will recede, as indistinct and gray
as those who hunted here,
as the rocky glacial scree,
that undergirds this cape,
flint under sand.

Solstice

Late June, the evening air
is full of forgiveness
and longing.

The yearly procession well begun,
old iris bracts curl into themselves,
fists of molten plastic,
ruched poppy petals litter and fall.

On this one lone long midsummer day
time stills itself,
one moment of relief
while we continue orbiting.

Tomorrow, on the slide down
towards July
a panic of growth sets in
all fragrance and rot.

So much to bear and be borne,
provided for, and then
made ready to move on

Each year the promenade the same
daylily and luna moth;
my human brain instead perceives
each season essentially more brief.

The Element Carbon

Carbon rarely acts alone,
Continually seeking combination.

Distant thunder now announces
Construction and destruction.

Fluidity of shape-shifter
And rigor of the form –
Both are admirable.

I was astonished
At carbon's gentle bellow
and scintillation.

The graphite mines of North Ontario
Would like to be revisited.

The depth and breadth of geologic time
Most wonderful.

An earthquake in slow motion
Altering the planet.

Soot falling from a chimney
In velvet flakes.

Cenozoic

Let the mastodon
slue pell-mell
across a field of nettles.
Eventually, an agate
tedium pervades
the grassy veldt
that will become
at some far distant time
our middle middle of America,
land of collies, cogs and wheels,
land of tactics,
world of marble visages
and malls.

Becalmed yet taut,
heat clogs the prairie's garbled density;
grass undulates
against the wind.
Tusks beckon like portals.
Above, in the present time, we gad about
in continuous motion, mad
as darning needles hovering
above a stagnant pond.
Our gathering motion does not indicate
how much of what we purchase is
simply, quietly, ill-gotten.

Whenever that iguana shows itself
our meager catboat on this inland sea
finds itself stranded
on the slowly moving continental plates
of our own extinction.

Samhain

Welcome, darkness
    running and laughing
        whispering fear away

Clouds creeping
    sky of black ink
        entering every cave and crack
           chill felt across the year.

Take an apple:
    look for life under the mask.
        Seeds are underground.

Experience
    the joyous brilliancy
        of sharp objects
           glimpsed through dark.

Fear not, exclaims the bonfire
    crouch down, unbend your knees.

    A single leaf touches ground.

Liquidity

Dusty scent of pinestraw
wheeze of chickadee
one red dragonfly
punctures my shirt shoulder.

From this point, downward

rain drums cabin walls
wakeful
in dry sleeping bag
with hill-stalking
thunder.

River Road

Annual breakup:
the ice jam moving
slowly out of Erie, lumpen-gray, downriver

past upright shingle-sided houses, lichen green,
Tonawanda's meager porches blank as early spring,
snow patches, gravel and slag.

The world is still half-toned,
like sepia rotogravure pictures of Black Rock Canal
with monster-headed railroad bridge
left crumpled on a Sunday afternoon.

We wiggle in the backseat of the old black Ford
and wonder why we do this every year,
when all there is to see is ice.

Grit-embedded, it growls, crunches,
charged with greasy imprint
spit from the refineries,
from Bethlehem Steel,
Republic Steel,
Dow Chemical,
the Chevy Stamping Plant
the brownblack fingerprint of labor.

We drive on to Grand Island
following River Road
ice everywhere, inexorable, along the shore
willow spines rattle, not yet yellow.

We are abjured to watch for
red flash of cardinal,
blackbirds perched on last year's reeds,
for one first glimpse of open water.

Across the river, bridges, squat refineries,
grain elevators, City Hall's art deco blunted dome,
the city's ragged skyline;
all the waterfront bars are open —
no more ice fishing this year. We drive.

Back in Tonawanda
empty picnic tables
dot the shore road,
bracts of grass push through old snow,
betray the nudging, pushing blocks.

Abe's drive-in ice cream place is open,
first weekend of the year,
we get cones that smell of summer
peppermint, pistachio, maple walnut.
There's a line behind us.

Ice squeals in the river.
Chilled teeth drive us to the car
to head home slowly
note one robin sitting in the snow
and count it spring.

Ice Age

Frost: comes in
flint chips,
gnarled whorls
grown bone,
coal plants
in eerie negative.

Second story windows rattle
locked in ghost frost.

Hawk and moon outside, reside apart,
ignore the other,
wind stories round house-seams,
seal us with shingles,
cement of story,
as Dad would read us to sleep.

Outside, glide of wingspread,
braking flutter,
settle, shrug, silence.
glare over shoulder;
absurd tiny head pivots,
glowers for prey.

And frost seals the house
apart from barns,
putty-thick, from neighbors.
It bandages windows,
turns prehistoric,
molecules clenched.

Living rooms collect
National Geographics, pictures,
paperbacks, dropped shoes, worn afghans,
television, pillows:
warm sediment of lives.

All wheels, waxes, wanes:
hawk, moon.
Dad the geologist
used to point out
condensation, glacial rock, mica,
stars, fossils, frost.